Brunch

RECIPES FOR COZY WEEKEND MORNINGS

recipes **Georgeanne Brennan**

photography **Laurie Frankel**

A Fireside Book
Published by Simon & Schuster
New York   London   Toronto   Sydney

contents

Brunch Entertaining

Brunch is an ideal meal for daytime entertaining for a variety of reasons. Because two meal periods are combined into one wonderful feast, guests feel they can indulge, leaving the host with many options for recipes. In addition, brunch is usually a casual get-together enjoyed on weekends and vacations when there are no strict timelines. Because of the informal setting and flexible menu, children can easily be included in the festivities, making brunch a great way to celebrate with family and friends of all ages.

CREATING THE OCCASION

Almost any occasion can be celebrated at a brunch, including birthdays, engagements, anniversaries, graduations, and the many other holidays and events that occur throughout the year. But brunch can also be enjoyed as an event all its own, for no other reason than the desire to share a relaxing afternoon with family and friends. If you are new to entertaining, brunch is a great meal to start with, as you only need to select one or two dishes for the menu. In addition, the recipes are typically easy to prepare. Happening as it does at the most relaxed time of the week, and featuring breakfast and light luncheon foods that are associated with comfort and leisure, brunch epitomizes both casual entertaining and festive celebrations.

SERVING STYLES

Brunch dishes lend themselves readily to informal presentations. For a small gathering of guests seated around a table, it's logical to serve the meal family-style: Bring the food out on serving platters from which guests can help themselves and pass the dish along. For large groups or to allow weekend guests to serve themselves at their own pace, a buffet is a

Keeping Foods Warm

To keep pancakes and waffles warm while you finish cooking all the batter, transfer the cooked items to a rack set over a baking sheet and put in a preheated 200°F oven until ready to serve. You can also use this method with sausage, bacon, and potatoes.

Make-Ahead Tip

When making pancakes, waffles, or quick breads, combine the dry ingredients in one bowl and pour the wet ingredients into another the night before you cook them. In the morning, simply whisk the ingredients together to make the batter.

good choice. Transform any tabletop into a buffet by stacking plates, flatware, napkins, and serving dishes on it. (For tips on setting up a brunch buffet, turn to page 90.) Of course, brunches do not always have to be casual affairs. When the occasion or your mood calls for it, you can make the meal as formal as you like, setting the table with your best linens, glassware, and tableware, and serving the food individually plated.

The versatility of brunch allows for great flexibility when it comes to where and how you serve it, if you choose to host a formal or informal meal, and whether you present the food on individual plates, family style, or as a buffet.

The dining room is one choice locale for brunch. Most tables will comfortably seat six to eight guests. For smaller gatherings, seating guests in a kitchen large enough to hold a table, or one with an adjoining breakfast nook, is an ideal way to make sure that everyone can mingle throughout the meal. This will create a relaxed mood and the proximity to the kitchen activities allows willing guests to assist you with the food.

There are other venues for brunch besides the predictable dining table. Living rooms can work well, especially if you are serving a large crowd or utilizing a buffet. Rearrange furniture as needed to provide convenient, comfortable seating; don't forget to include tables for guests to rest their plates.

If the weather is warm, consider serving the meal outside. Set up the buffet near a door with easy outdoor access or in the yard on a table that is protected from sunlight. Be sure to position tables, chairs, or blankets on

the lawn beneath umbrellas or trees to shade your guests while they eat.

PLANNING THE MENU

Remember that brunch doesn't need to be a multicourse affair. One hearty dish, such as Steak & Eggs (page 75), can be more than enough. Alternatively, adding a starter or baked item can make for an elegant, lingering event. Also, the occasion, guest list, and season will help you determine the best menu choices. If the your guest list will include children, consider serving waffles, pancakes, or the kid-friendly Croque-Monsieur (page 87). A celebratory meal could feature a more upscale main dish, such as Salmon Eggs Benedict (page 49). During the spring, when asparagus is at its peak, serve Spring Vegetable Frittata (page 35). If you are hosting a brunch for a holiday during the cold winter months,

Tips for Successful Brunch Entertaining

- Pick a serving style—formal or informal, individually plated, family style, or buffet—that matches your mood, the number of guests, and any time constraints.

- Select a location that's right for the style of the brunch and the season—in the dining room, in an eat-in kitchen, in the garden, or in a large living room.

- Choose a menu that combines make-ahead dishes with last-minute preparations; use the season or the weather and the preferences of your guests to help you make decisions about your menu selections.

- The night before the brunch, clean the house, set the table, choose the serving vessels and utensils, and do as much advance cooking as you can.

- If you are serving a brunch outdoors, consider supplying mesh domes to keep bugs away from the food.

- For a pretty finishing touch, choose a simple centerpiece or floral arrangement to create a focal point for your meal. For smaller tables or meals served at the kitchen counter, put an individual bloom in a bud vase at each place setting.

Baked-Goods Station

Fill plates or napkin-lined baskets with Oatmeal-Blueberry Muffins (page 65), Orange-Zest Scones (page 64), or Brown-Sugar Coffee Cake (page 62), or serve purchased breads and bagels. Position the items near an electrical outlet where a toaster can be plugged in safely. Add bowls of toppings so guests can help themselves.

Cereal Buffet

Place containers of homemade granola (page 29) or a favorite dry cereal on a counter with serving spoons. Offer flavored yogurt such as Orange-Blossom Yogurt (page 29) and a pitcher of milk. Supplement these with bowls of dried fruit and toasted nuts. Stack bowls, spoons, and napkins nearby.

choose a more substantial dish such as Red Flannel Hash (page 77) or Sausage & Cheddar Strata (page 83).

As for beverages, there are a profusion of appropriate brunch choices. Hot drinks such as freshly brewed coffee or tea are classic standbys, but consider including other warm beverages such as Mexican Hot Chocolate (page 113) or Chai Tea Latte (page 114), too. For a special touch, serve Sparkling Ginger Lemonade (page 110). If you want to serve cocktails as well, try a Spiced Bloody Mary (page 119) or a Classic Bellini (page 117). For more drink ideas, turn to pages 108–119.

Cooking is easier if you pair dishes that are prepared at the last minute with those that can be made ahead of time. It is also a good idea to balance your brunch menu with a combination of both savory and sweet dishes. Recipes rich in butter or cheese are best served with those that feature fruit, for example. Finally, be sure to offer meatless dishes for vegetarians and nonalcoholic beverages for nondrinkers and children.

SETTING THE SCENE

Set the table the night before you entertain so that you will have more time the next morning to prepare the meal and visit with your arriving guests. Choose serving vessels that complement the shapes and colors of the food and appropriate serving utensils.

Simple bouquets of seasonal flowers or baskets or bowls of fruits featured in the menu are all that are needed for attractive,

easy-to-make centerpieces. To complete the mood, play music that suits the tastes of your guests, keeping it at a low volume so it won't interfere with conversations. For more tips on creating a simple centerpiece and setting a brunch table, turn to pages 18 and 32.

PUTTING IT ALL TOGETHER

Always remember that the main reason for entertaining is to share a happy occasion with your guests. If you know that some of your guests enjoy cooking, ask them to help with some of the last-minute kitchen tasks. If children are going to be present, have on hand some kid-friendly activities for them to enjoy while the adults are conversing. A croquet set, playing cards, or a board game can be fun for guests of all ages and can be used to entertain everyone before or after the meal is enjoyed.

Regardless of whether you serve the meal at the table or from a buffet, consider setting up stations where guests can help themselves to baked goods or cereals (page 12), juices (top right), and cocktails (page 108). These are especially useful ideas when you are hosting weekend houseguests and have multiple meal periods to plan.

Self-Service Juice Bar

For a casual brunch, place a bowlful of chilled, halved oranges or grapefruits on a buffet or kitchen counter alongside an electric juicer or manual juice press. Guests can squeeze a glass of fresh juice for themselves.

Beverage Bar

Hand squeeze one or more citrus juices such as orange, blood orange, or grapefruit, or purchase freshly squeezed juices from the store. Pour the juices into glass pitchers and refrigerate until well chilled. When you're ready to serve, arrange the pitchers of juice on a sideboard or counter with small juice glasses. Provide sparkling water and ice cubes in case guests wish to make citrus spritzers.

Whether you are cooking for your family, enjoying a weekend with an intimate group, or hosting a crowd for a special occasion, brunch is the perfect way to entertain. With a little bit of advance planning and a well-considered menu, all you need for your next brunch party is to set the date.

starters

Tips for a Brunch Centerpiece

A centerpiece can be the decorative focal point of a brunch table. Keep it low and simple so that it does not obstruct the line of sight or overwhelm the food.

Choose a low vase or other container that will allow the guests to converse easily across the table once it is filled. Make sure it has a wide base for stability.

Fill the vessel two-thirds full with citrus fruits, river stones, or beach glass. Add lukewarm water to come halfway up the sides of the vase.

Insert the flowers into the vase one stem at a time, using the fruits or stones to anchor the stems.

Aim for a pleasing shape and balance of color. If you are using a variety of flowers, insert the largest ones first, then fill in with the smaller ones.

Citrus Salad

Here, buttery Spanish Marcona almonds, available in specialty-food stores, contrast nicely with the sweet Medjool dates and tangy citrus used in this wintertime salad. If you like, you can substitute burgundy-fleshed blood oranges for the navel oranges.

In a large bowl, combine the olive oil, grapefruit juice, vinegar, salt, and pepper and mix well with a fork to make a vinaigrette.

Working with 1 grapefruit at a time, and using a large knife, cut off a slice from the top and bottom of the fruit to expose the flesh. Stand the grapefruit on a flat end and, following the curve of the fruit, cut away all the peel and white pith. Working over a clean bowl, cut along both sides of each segment to free it from the membrane and let it fall into the bowl. Repeat to section the oranges. Using the tip of a knife, dislodge and discard any seeds in the citrus segments, then cut the segments in half. (The citrus fruits can be sectioned up to 4 hours in advance, covered, and refrigerated until you are ready to continue.)

Using a slotted spoon, transfer the citrus segments to the bowl with the vinaigrette. Add half of the dates and the arugula leaves. Gently toss the ingredients to coat them with the vinaigrette.

Divide the salad evenly among chilled salad plates, garnish with the remaining dates and the almonds, and serve right away.

SERVES 4–6

Extra-virgin olive oil, 2 tablespoons

Fresh grapefruit juice, 1 tablespoon

Raspberry vinegar, ½ teaspoon

Sea salt or kosher salt, ¼ teaspoon

Freshly ground pepper, ¼ teaspoon

Grapefruits, 2

Navel or Valencia oranges, 3

Medjool dates, 6, each pitted and cut lengthwise into 6 pieces

Small arugula leaves, 1 cup

Marcona almonds, 2 tablespoons

Fresh Berry Salad with Mint

This simple salad makes a perfect addition to a brunch held during the summer months. Small spinach leaves provide a crisp and colorful counterpoint to the soft-textured blue and red berries, while the honey-lemon dressing brings out their sweetness.

Honey, 1 teaspoon

Fresh lemon juice,
2 teaspoons

Fresh blueberries, 1 cup

Fresh blackberries, 1 cup

Fresh raspberries, 1 cup

Fresh mint,
2 tablespoons chopped

Small spinach leaves,
1 cup

In a small bowl, combine the honey and lemon juice and mix well with a whisk to make a dressing. Set aside. In a bowl, combine the blueberries, blackberries, raspberries, and mint.

Pour the honey-lemon dressing over the berries and mint and, using a large spoon, mix gently, taking care not to break the berries. Add the spinach leaves and mix gently again.

Divide the salad evenly among chilled salad plates. Serve right away.

SERVES 4–6

Green Salad with Almonds

Mixed salad greens, readily available in a variety of combinations, often include mildly bitter varieties, such as radicchio, escarole, and arugula. Here, the pleasing bitterness is tempered by toasted nuts and a tangy-sweet vinaigrette made with Champagne vinegar and honey.

Preheat the oven to 350°F. Spread the almonds in a single layer on a rimmed baking sheet. Toast in the oven, stirring once or twice, until pale gold and fragrant, about 15 minutes. Transfer to a plate and let cool completely. (The nuts can be toasted up to 3 days in advance and stored in an airtight container at room temperature.)

In a large bowl, combine the olive oil, vinegar, honey, salt, and pepper and mix with a fork to make a vinaigrette. Add the salad greens and toss to coat evenly with the vinaigrette. Add all but 1 tablespoon of the toasted almonds and toss again.

Divide the salad evenly among chilled salad plates, garnish with the chives and the reserved almonds, and serve right away.

SERVES 4–6

Whole almonds, ½ cup

Extra-virgin olive oil,
3 tablespoons

Champagne vinegar,
1 tablespoon

Honey, 1 teaspoon

Sea salt or kosher salt,
½ teaspoon

Freshly ground white pepper, ¼ teaspoon

Small mixed salad greens, 5 cups

Fresh chives,
1 tablespoon minced

Warm Spinach Salad

The nutty flavor and smooth, firm texture of golden chanterelle mushrooms make them an excellent addition to this warm salad. Their seasoned cooking juices are a flavorful base for the dressing. You can rinse, dry, and refrigerate the spinach leaves the night before serving.

Extra-virgin olive oil, 3 tablespoons

Shallot, 2 teaspoons minced

Garlic, 1 clove, minced

Chanterelle mushrooms, $\frac{1}{2}$ pound, brushed clean and cut lengthwise into quarters

Sea salt or kosher salt, $\frac{1}{2}$ teaspoon

Freshly ground pepper, $\frac{1}{2}$ teaspoon

Sherry vinegar, 1 tablespoon

Spinach leaves, 6 cups (about 2 bunches), stems removed

In a frying pan over medium heat, warm 2 tablespoons of the olive oil. Add the shallot, garlic, mushrooms, and $\frac{1}{4}$ teaspoon of the salt. Sauté until the mushrooms are golden and soft, 4–5 minutes. Remove from the heat, and, using a slotted spoon, transfer the mushroom mixture to a bowl, cover with aluminum foil to keep warm, and set aside. Leave the drippings in the pan.

To make the dressing, return the pan to medium heat and add the remaining 1 tablespoon olive oil and $\frac{1}{4}$ teaspoon salt, the pepper, and the vinegar to make a dressing. Heat, stirring, just until hot, about 1 minute, then pour into a large bowl.

Add the spinach to the bowl and toss to coat evenly with the dressing. Add the reserved mushroom mixture and toss again until the ingredients are evenly distributed.

Divide the salad evenly among salad plates and serve right away.

SERVES 4–6

Cucumber Gazpacho

Serrano chiles add a touch of heat to this sophisticated cold soup. For a bit of tomato flavor without changing the color, add peeled and seeded green heirloom tomatoes, such as two Green Zebras or a handful of Green Grape tomatoes, to the blender with the cucumbers.

Nonfat plain yogurt, 1½ cups

Day-old baguette, 3 slices, torn into 1-inch pieces

Cucumbers, 6, peeled, halved, seeded, and coarsely chopped (about 6 cups)

Sherry vinegar, 1 tablespoon

Sea salt or kosher salt, ½–1 teaspoon

Fresh lemon juice, 1 tablespoon

Serrano chiles, 2, seeded and coarsely chopped

Red or green bell pepper, 1, seeded and coarsely chopped

Fresh chives, 3 tablespoons chopped plus whole chives, cut into 4-inch lengths, for garnish

In a bowl, combine the yogurt and bread pieces, stirring lightly to mix. Let stand for about 10 minutes to allow the bread to soften.

Meanwhile, put the cucumbers in a blender and purée until smooth. Add the yogurt and bread, vinegar, salt, lemon juice, chiles, bell pepper, and chopped chives and purée until smooth. (You may need to purée the soup in 2 batches to avoid spills.) Pour into a large bowl, cover, and refrigerate for at least 4 hours or up to overnight to chill thoroughly and blend the flavors.

Divide the soup evenly among chilled bowls and garnish with the whole chives, crossing them over each other. Serve right away.

SERVES 6–8

Lox & Bagel Bar

Nothing could be simpler than to start a brunch with a welcoming spread of bagels, lox, cream cheese, and condiments. Arrange the ingredients so that the guests can help themselves, leaving you free to prepare the rest of the meal or pour drinks.

Clear a wide serving area, such as a sideboard, a kitchen counter, or a table. If desired, cover it with a tablecloth or place mats.

Carefully cut the bagels in half horizontally and toast them if you wish. Place the bagels in a napkin-lined basket and put the basket at the far left of the serving area.

Spoon the cream cheese into a small bowl and set it, along with 1 or 2 spreaders, to the right of the bagels. Arrange the lox on a platter, separating the slices slightly so that they are easy to pick up. Set the lox platter, with a serving fork or two, to the right of the cream cheese.

Put the capers in a second small bowl, and the onion in a third. Put the lemon wedges on a plate. Place these items to the right of the lox, along with the appropriate serving utensils (spoons for the capers and onion, and a couple of forks for the lemons).

Invite your guests to serve themselves (working from left to right at the buffet), first spreading a bagel half with cream cheese, then topping it with the lox, and finally adding the condiments of choice.

SERVES 6–8

Bagels in assorted flavors, 12

Whipped cream cheese, 1 pound

Lox, ¾ pound thinly sliced

Capers, 1 cup, well-drained

Red onion, 2 cups minced

Lemons, 3, each cut into 6 wedges

Granola & Yogurt Parfait

This crunchy, honey-laced granola can be made up to one week in advance, giving you extra time to put together other dishes the morning of the brunch. Plain yogurt enhanced with orange-flower water and orange zest makes an easy but elegant accompaniment.

To make the granola, preheat the oven to 300°F. In a large bowl, combine the oats, millet, sunflower seeds, pecans, almonds, oil, honey, brown sugar, cinnamon, and vanilla extract. Using a wooden spoon, mix the ingredients until evenly distributed; the mixture will be stiff and sticky.

Spread the granola mixture on a large rimmed baking sheet and place in the oven. Bake, stirring from time to time, until browned and crisp, 45–60 minutes. Remove from the oven and let cool completely. When cool, break apart any clumped bits of granola. (You can store the granola in an airtight container at room temperature for up to 1 week.)

To make the orange-blossom yogurt, put the yogurt in a bowl. Add the orange-flower water and orange zest and mix well. (The yogurt can be mixed up to 1 day ahead of time and refrigerated.)

Divide the granola evenly among small bowls. Pour the yogurt over the top, dividing evenly, and serve right away.

MAKES ABOUT 4 1/2 CUPS; SERVES 4–6

GRANOLA

Old-fashioned rolled oats, 2 cups

Yellow millet, 1/2 cup

Shelled sunflower seeds, 1 cup

Chopped pecans, 1/2 cup

Chopped almonds, 1/2 cup

Canola oil, 1/2 cup

Floral honey, 1/2 cup

Light brown sugar, 3 tablespoons firmly packed

Ground cinnamon, 1 teaspoon

Vanilla extract, 1 teaspoon

ORANGE-BLOSSOM YOGURT

Nonfat plain yogurt, 1 1/2 cups

Orange-flower water, 2 teaspoons

Orange zest, 2 teaspoons finely grated

egg dishes

Tips for Setting the Brunch Table

A well pulled together table can reflect the mood of the occasion—even a casual brunch—and helps make the meal a comfortable and memorable experience.

Select a pretty tablecloth or attractive place mats and complementary napkins. Fold the napkins neatly and place them on top of or to the left of each plate.

Position the flatware in the order in which they will be used, working from the outside in. Place the forks on the left, and the knife, blade inward, and a spoon, if needed, to the right of the plate.

Arrange the glassware to the right above the knife. Place a small spoon on the coffee cup's saucer.

Create an interesting detail such as placing a flower on top of each napkin or a hand-written place card on each plate.

Spring Vegetable Frittata

Vary the cheeses, vegetables, and herbs to customize this dish to your own taste. This frittata, redolent with asparagus, cherry tomatoes, and goat cheese, can be made up to one hour in advance and kept at room temperature until you are ready to serve it.

Bring 1 inch of water to a boil in a steamer pan. Place the asparagus in the steamer rack, set over the boiling water, cover, and steam until the asparagus can be easily pierced with a fork, 4–5 minutes. Remove from the steamer and plunge into a bowl of ice water for 4–5 minutes to halt the cooking. Drain, cut into ½-inch pieces, and set aside.

Preheat the broiler and position a rack 8 inches from the heat source. In a bowl, combine the eggs, half-and-half, cheese, salt, and pepper and whisk until evenly distributed, about 2 minutes.

In a 14-inch ovenproof frying pan, melt the butter with the olive oil. When the butter foams, add the shallot and sauté until softened, 2–3 minutes. Quickly layer the asparagus pieces and the tomatoes in the pan and pour the egg mixture over them. Reduce the heat to low and cook just until the eggs are set around the edges, 3–4 minutes. Using a heatproof rubber spatula, lift the edge and tip the pan so the uncooked egg runs underneath. Place the pan under the broiler and cook until the top of the frittata is set and a knife inserted into the center comes out clean, 4–5 minutes.

Remove the frittata from the broiler and sprinkle with the tarragon. Cut into wedges and serve hot, warm, or at room temperature.

SERVES 4–6

Asparagus spears,
16, tough ends removed

Large or extra-large eggs, 8, lightly beaten

Half-and-half,
2 tablespoons

Fresh goat cheese,
2 ounces, crumbled

Sea salt or kosher salt,
½ teaspoon

Freshly ground pepper,
½ teaspoon

Unsalted butter,
1 tablespoon

Extra-virgin olive oil,
1 tablespoon

Shallot, 2 tablespoons minced

Cherry tomatoes,
½ cup stemmed and halved

Fresh tarragon,
1 tablespoon minced

Piperade & Poached Eggs

Piperade, a classic Basque dish featuring sweet peppers, onions, and tomatoes, is used here as a flavorful base for poached eggs. *Piment d'Espelette* is a fiery chile from the Basque region. It is typically dried, ground, and sold in tins at specialty-food stores.

Extra-virgin olive oil,
2 tablespoons

Yellow onion, 1 large,
minced

Red bell pepper,
1 large, seeded and
thinly sliced crosswise
into rings

Green bell pepper,
1 large, seeded and
thinly sliced crosswise
into rings

Ripe, juicy tomatoes,
4, peeled, seeded, and
coarsely chopped

Garlic, 1 clove, minced

Sea salt or kosher salt,
½ teaspoon

**Freshly ground black
pepper,** ¼ teaspoon

Piment d'Espelette **or
cayenne pepper,**
¼ teaspoon

**Large or extra-large
eggs,** 4

In a frying pan over medium heat, warm the olive oil. Add the onion and sauté until translucent, 2–3 minutes. Add the red and green bell peppers and sauté until they begin to soften, 3–4 minutes. Cover and cook until the vegetables are very soft and limp, 3–4 minutes more. Stir in the tomatoes, garlic, salt, black pepper, and *piment d'Espelette*. Re-cover, reduce the heat to low, and cook until the mixture thickens, about 20 minutes. Keep the mixture warm. (The piperade can be made up to 2 days in advance, covered, and refrigerated. Reheat gently just before serving.)

Poach the eggs as directed on page 38.

To serve, divide the piperade among warmed individual bowls and top each serving with a poached egg. Serve right away.

SERVES 4

Poached Eggs

Poached eggs are a versatile brunch staple. Serve them as is with a couple of side dishes, or pair them with other morning favorites such as Salmon Eggs Benedict (page 49) or Red Flannel Hash (page 77). For the best results, use the freshest eggs available.

Fresh lemon juice,
1 teaspoon

Large or extra-large eggs, 8

Sea salt or kosher salt

Freshly ground pepper

Fill a large sauté pan with water to a depth of 2 inches and add the lemon juice. Place over medium heat and bring just to a simmer. Break 1 egg into a small bowl or cup and gently slip it into the simmering water. Quickly repeat with the remaining eggs, keeping them about 1 inch apart. Reduce the heat to low and simmer gently, basting the eggs occasionally with spoonfuls of the water, until the whites are set and the yolks are glazed over but still soft, 4–5 minutes.

Using a skimmer or slotted spatula, remove the eggs from the water, drain briefly on paper towels, and trim any ragged edges from the whites with a knife or kitchen scissors. Slide the eggs onto plates, season to taste with salt and pepper, and serve right away.

SERVES 4

Ham & Cheddar Omelet

The favorite combination of ham and cheese comes together here in a simple omelet. To complete the menu, offer Potato Pancakes (page 100) or Roasted Spiced Apples (page 94), and Blood Orange Mimosas (page 116).

Break the eggs into a bowl. Add the salt and pepper and beat with a fork until the whites and yolks are blended.

In a 14-inch nonstick frying pan over medium heat, melt the butter. When the butter foams, add the eggs and stir slowly with a heatproof rubber spatula until the eggs begin to thicken, just a few seconds, then reduce the heat to low. As the eggs cook and set along the edges, lift the set portions with the spatula and tip the pan to allow the uncooked egg to run underneath. Continue to cook, lift, and tip until the eggs are set, about 1 minute for a softer texture or about 20 seconds longer for a firmer texture.

Sprinkle the ham, cheese, and green onions on one half of the omelet, leaving a 1-inch border along the edge. Slip the spatula under the uncovered half and flip it over to cover the fillings. Cook for another 30–40 seconds to heat the fillings.

Slide the omelet onto a warmed platter. Using a large knife, cut the omelet crosswise into 2- to 3-inch pieces and serve right away.

SERVES 4–6

Large or extra-large eggs, 8

Sea salt or kosher salt, ½ teaspoon

Freshly ground pepper, ½ teaspoon

Unsalted butter, 1½ tablespoons

Smoked ham, ½ pound, cut into ½-inch cubes

White Cheddar cheese, ¼ pound, shredded

Green onions, 4, with 2 inches of tender green tops, finely chopped

Huevos Rancheros

It is well worth the effort to make this classic ranchero sauce, which gets its smoky bite from ancho chiles. You can make the sauce up to two days in advance, let it cool completely, and then refrigerate it in an airtight container. Accompany with your favorite beans and rice.

In a heatproof bowl, combine the broth and chiles. Soak the chiles until soft, 8–10 minutes. Drain the chiles, reserving the broth. Tear off the stem ends from the chiles and discard. Slit the chiles lengthwise, scrape out and discard the seeds, and coarsely chop the flesh. Set aside.

In a large frying pan over medium-high heat, warm 2 tablespoons of the oil. When the oil is hot, add the onion and sauté until translucent, 2–3 minutes. Add the garlic and sauté just until soft, about 1 minute. Remove from the heat.

In a blender or food processor, combine the chopped chiles, sautéed onion and garlic, tomatoes and their juice, half of the oregano, and the cumin. Process to a smooth purée, then pour into the pan. Place over medium heat and cook, stirring, until it thickens and bubbles, about 2 minutes. Add salt to taste, the chipotle, and about ½ cup of the reserved broth. Cook for 1–2 minutes, then taste and adjust the seasoning. Continue to cook, stirring occasionally, until the sauce is thick but pourable, 1–2 minutes. Keep warm.

Fry the eggs sunny-side up or over easy as directed on page 42.

For each serving, put 2 eggs on a warmed plate with 1–2 spoonfuls of the sauce. Serve right away, accompanied by the tortillas.

SERVES 4

Beef broth, 1 cup, boiling

Ancho chiles, 3

Corn or canola oil, 5 tablespoons

White onion, ½ cup chopped

Garlic, 2 cloves, minced

Whole tomatoes, 1 can (28 ounces)

Fresh oregano, 1 tablespoon, or 1 teaspoon dried oregano

Ground cumin, ½ teaspoon

Sea salt or kosher salt, ½–1 teaspoon

Ground chipotle chile, ½ teaspoon

Large or extra-large eggs, 8

Corn or flour tortillas, 8, warmed

Fried Eggs

Featuring fried eggs on a brunch menu means you can customize the cooking to the tastes of your guests. Ask if they prefer their eggs sunny-side up (with a clear, bright yellow yolk) or over easy (with a yolk that has a slightly opaque film).

Unsalted butter or canola oil, 2 tablespoons

Large or extra-large eggs, 8

Sea salt or kosher salt

Freshly ground pepper

For eggs cooked sunny-side up, melt the butter in a large frying pan over medium-high heat. When the butter foams, break the eggs into the pan, spacing them about 1 inch apart. Reduce the heat to low and sprinkle the eggs with salt and pepper to taste. Cover the pan and cook until the whites are set and the yolks begin to firm around the edges, 5–7 minutes. Using a slotted metal spatula, transfer the eggs to individual plates and serve right away.

For eggs cooked over easy, melt the butter in a large frying pan over medium-high heat. When the butter foams, break the eggs into the pan, spacing them about 1 inch apart. Reduce the heat to low and sprinkle the eggs with salt and pepper to taste. Cook until the whites are set and the yolks begin to firm around the edges, 5–7 minutes. Using a slotted metal spatula, turn over the eggs and cook just until the yolks form an opaque film, 30–45 seconds. (For a firmer yolk, cook for 1–1½ minutes on the second side.) Transfer the eggs to individual plates and serve right away.

SERVES 4

Smoky Vegetable Scramble

Green garlic flavors this simple scramble laced with smoky Gouda cheese and sweet red peppers. If you can't find green garlic, a regular garlic clove can be used. Round out this dish with a side of Herbed Pork Sausages (page 103) or a platter of fresh fruit.

Cut off and discard the green stalks from the green garlic. Remove the coarse outer skin from the bulb and then mince the bulb. (If using a garlic clove, peel it, halve it lengthwise, remove and discard the bitter green sprout at its center, and mince.) Set aside.

Break the eggs into a bowl. Add the salt and pepper and beat with a fork until the whites and yolks are blended.

In a frying pan over medium heat, melt the butter. When the butter foams, add the minced garlic and bell pepper and sauté until the garlic is translucent, 2–3 minutes. Pour in the eggs, then reduce the heat to low. Cook, stirring intermittently with a heatproof rubber spatula for larger curds, or frequently for smaller curds, until the eggs are cooked to the desired consistency, about 5 minutes for a soft texture, or 7–8 minutes for a firmer one. Stir in the cheese and parsley about 2 minutes before the eggs are done to your liking.

Spoon the eggs onto a warmed platter and serve right away.

SERVES 4–6

Green garlic, 2 stalks, or 1 clove garlic

Extra-large eggs, 8

Sea salt or kosher salt, ½ teaspoon

Freshly ground pepper, ½ teaspoon

Unsalted butter, 2 tablespoons

Red bell pepper, 1, seeded and finely chopped

Smoked Gouda cheese, ¼ pound, cubed

Fresh flat-leaf parsley, 2 tablespoons minced

Scrambled Eggs

Scrambled eggs are an excellent addition to any brunch menu, whether they are served on individual plates with side dishes, such as Crispy Pepper Bacon (page 102) and Roasted Rosemary Potatoes (page 96), or as a part of a larger, buffet-style meal.

Break the eggs into a bowl. Add the salt and pepper and beat with a fork until the whites and yolks are blended.

In a large frying pan over medium heat, melt the butter. When the butter foams, reduce the heat to low. Add the eggs and cook, stirring intermittently with a heatproof rubber spatula for larger curds, or frequently for smaller curds, until the eggs are cooked to the desired consistency, 4–5 minutes for a soft texture, and 7–8 minutes for a firmer one.

Spoon the eggs onto a warmed platter and serve right away.

SERVES 4

Large or extra-large eggs, 8

Sea salt or kosher salt, ½ teaspoon

Freshly ground pepper, ½ teaspoon

Unsalted butter, 2 tablespoons

Baked Eggs with Spinach

These classic French eggs are elegantly presented in their cooking ramekins, so choose attractive vessels to complement your table setting. For a variation, replace the bed of spinach with Piperade (page 36), using about one-half cup for each ramekin.

Unsalted butter,
1 tablespoon plus
2 teaspoons

Spinach, 1½ pounds
(about 2 bunches), large
stems removed

Sea salt or kosher salt,
1½ teaspoons

**Large or extra-large
eggs,** 4

Freshly ground pepper,
¼ teaspoon

Heavy cream,
4 teaspoons

Preheat the oven to 350°F. Rub the inside of four ½-cup ramekins with the 1 tablespoon butter.

Fill a large pot three-fourths full with water, bring to a boil over high heat, and add 1 teaspoon of the salt. Drop in the spinach and cook until limp and tender but still bright green, about 4 minutes. Drain through a colander and immediately rinse under running cold water to halt the cooking. Drain well and squeeze firmly to remove excess water. Coarsely chop the spinach. (The spinach can be cooked, cooled, and chopped up to 1 day in advance; cover and refrigerate until needed.)

Divide the chopped spinach evenly among the prepared ramekins, making a bed in the bottom. Dot each bed with ½ teaspoon of the remaining butter, cut into bits. Break an egg into each ramekin. Sprinkle the eggs with the remaining ½ teaspoon salt and the pepper, dividing evenly. Drizzle each egg with 1 teaspoon of the cream. Arrange the ramekins on a rimmed baking sheet.

Bake the eggs until the whites are set and the yolks are firm around the edges and soft in the center, about 15 minutes. Remove from the oven and serve right away.

SERVES 4–6

Salmon Eggs Benedict

Eggs Benedict, gilded with butter-rich hollandaise sauce, is a quintessential special-occasion brunch dish. In this recipe, smoked salmon is substituted for the traditional Canadian bacon and a ripe tomato is added for a different spin on the classic.

To make the hollandaise, in a saucepan over medium heat, melt the butter. Remove from the heat and keep warm. In a small nonaluminum saucepan, warm the lemon juice over low heat. Pour water to a depth of about 1 inch into the bottom part of a double boiler and bring to a low simmer. Add the egg yolks to the top part of the double boiler and place over, but not touching, the barely simmering water. Cook the yolks, whisking constantly until they begin to thicken, about 3–4 minutes, then add 1 tablespoon of the boiling water. Continue to whisk until the yolks thicken, 1–2 more seconds. Whisk in 1 tablespoon of the boiling water, and continue whisking to thicken. Repeat twice, adding 1 tablespoon boiling water each time. Whisk in the warmed lemon juice and remove the pan from the heat. Very slowly pour in the melted butter while whisking constantly. Whisk in the salt and cayenne pepper and keep whisking until the sauce triples in volume, 3–4 more minutes.

Poach the eggs as directed on page 38.

For each serving, toast 2 English muffin halves and place, cut side up, on a warmed plate. Top each half with 1 tomato slice, one-eighth of the smoked salmon, and 1 egg. Spoon 2 tablespoons of the hollandaise sauce over each egg, garnish with the chives, and serve right away.

SERVES 4

HOLLANDAISE SAUCE

Unsalted butter, 1/2 cup

Fresh lemon juice, 1 1/2 tablespoons

Large egg yolks, 3

Boiling water, 4 tablespoons

Sea salt or kosher salt, 1/4 teaspoon

Cayenne pepper, 1/4 teaspoon

Large eggs, 8

English muffins, 4, halved

Tomato slices, 8

Fresh chives, chopped for garnish

Smoked salmon, 1/2 pound thinly sliced

morning sweets

Tips for Making the Perfect Pot of Tea

Making great tea is easy if you remember a few key steps: start with cold, fresh spring water; warm the teapot first; and use high-quality loose tea instead of tea bags.

Warm the teapot by pouring a small amount of boiling spring water into it, swirling the water, letting it sit for a minute or two, and then pouring it out.

Add loose-leaf tea to the pot, allowing 1 teaspoon for each person, plus 1 extra teaspoon for the pot. Pour in 1 cup boiling spring water per person.

Cover the pot and let the tea steep for 2–7 minutes, depending on the type of tea and how strong you prefer it. Strain the brewed tea into teacups.

Set out the accompaniments—milk, sugar cubes, and lemon slices—for serving. Have a napkin-lined plate nearby to place the strainer after pouring.

Buttermilk Waffles

These waffles are a perennial brunch favorite and a great addition to your menu. If some of your guests are children, you can serve them with butter and syrup instead of the compote. Every waffle iron is different, so be sure you are familiar with the manufacturer's directions.

Preheat a waffle iron following the manufacturer's directions. In a large bowl, whisk together the flour, baking powder, baking soda, and salt. In another bowl, whisk the egg yolks until blended, then whisk in the buttermilk and the 5 tablespoons melted butter. Add the yolk mixture to the flour mixture and whisk until a smooth batter forms.

In a bowl, using a handheld electric mixer, beat the egg whites and sugar until stiff peaks form, about 2 minutes. Using a rubber spatula, gently fold the whites into the batter until incorporated.

Lightly brush the waffle iron with melted butter. Pour enough batter for 1 waffle into the preheated waffle iron. Using a rubber spatula, quickly spread the batter to within 1/4 inch of the edge of the iron. Close the lid and do not disturb for at least 1 minute. Cook the waffle until no steam is visible and the lid opens easily, 3–5 minutes, or according to the manufacturer's directions. Using a spatula, remove the waffle from the iron, place on a warmed platter, and cover with aluminum foil to keep warm. Repeat until all of the batter has been used.

Divide the waffles among individual plates, top with the Strawberry-Rhubarb Compote, and serve right away.

MAKES 12 WAFFLES; SERVES 6–8

All-purpose flour, 2 1/2 cups

Baking powder, 2 1/4 teaspoons

Baking soda, 1/2 teaspoon

Salt, 1/2 teaspoon

Large or extra-large eggs, 3, separated

Buttermilk, 2 cups

Unsalted butter, 5 tablespoons, melted and slightly cooled, plus more melted butter for cooking

Sugar, 2 teaspoons

Strawberry-Rhubarb Compote (page 56)

Strawberry-Rhubarb Compote

This compote is almost jamlike and makes a delicious accompaniment to Buttermilk Waffles (page 55). The longer the rhubarb cooks, the more it breaks down; the relatively short cooking time here ensures the bite-sized rhubarb chunks will remain intact.

Rhubarb, 5 stalks, ends trimmed, strings removed, and stalks cut into ½-inch pieces

Sugar, ⅓ cup

Strawberries, 1 pound (about 2 pints), hulled and halved lengthwise

Fresh lemon juice, 1 teaspoon

In a nonaluminum saucepan, combine the rhubarb and sugar and let stand for 30 minutes. Place the pan over medium heat and cook, stirring often. During the first few minutes of cooking, the rhubarb will release its juices. If the mixture looks dry, stir in 2–3 teaspoons water. Continue to cook until the rhubarb pieces are soft but not dissolving, about 8 minutes total. During the final 3 minutes of cooking, stir in the strawberries and lemon juice.

Remove the compote from the heat and let cool, about 10 minutes. (The compote can be made up to 2 days in advance. Let cool completely, then cover tightly and refrigerate.) Serve the compote warm or at room temperature.

MAKES ABOUT 4 CUPS

Stuffed French Toast

French toast can be savory, with a sprinkle of salt and pepper, or sweet, with the addition of jam. This version falls between the two, with the cream cheese contributing the savory element and the citrus marmalade adding its fruity sweetness.

Break the eggs into a shallow bowl, add the sugar and salt, and beat with a fork until the whites and yolks are blended. In a large frying pan over medium heat, melt 4 tablespoons of butter. When the butter foams, immerse the bread slices, one at a time, in the beaten eggs and then place them in the hot pan, adding as many as will fit without crowding. Cook until lightly golden on the bottom, about 4 minutes. Using a spatula, turn them over and cook until the second side is lightly golden, about 4 minutes more. Transfer the toasts to a warmed platter and cover with aluminum foil to keep warm. Repeat with the remaining slices, adding more butter as needed to prevent sticking.

Spread 4 of the slices with a layer of cream cheese, dividing it evenly. Then spread a layer of marmalade over the cream cheese, again dividing it evenly. Top with the remaining 4 slices.

Return the frying pan to medium heat, adding more butter as needed to prevent sticking. When the butter foams, place the filled French toasts in the pan and cook just until the bottom is golden brown, about 1 minute. Gently flip the toasts and cook the other sides until golden brown, about 1 minute more. Transfer to warmed individual plates and serve right away.

SERVES 4

Large or extra-large eggs, 5

Sugar, 1 teaspoon

Salt, ¼ teaspoon

Unsalted butter, 4–6 tablespoons

Whole-wheat or white bread, 8 slices

Cream cheese, ½ pound at room temperature

Citrus marmalade such as orange, kumquat, or Meyer lemon, ½ cup

French Toast & Apple Chutney

This old-fashioned French toast is made with egg-rich brioche. A side of homemade apple chutney, sweetened with dried fruits and a dessert wine, is the perfect accompaniment. Serve this hearty autumn dish with Crispy Pepper Bacon (page 102).

APPLE CHUTNEY

Granny Smith apples, 8, peeled, cored, and cut into 1-inch cubes

Golden raisins, ½ cup

Dried figs, ¼ cup chopped

Light brown sugar, 1 cup firmly packed

Late-harvest Riesling, or other sweet dessert wine, 1 cup

Lemon zest, 1 tablespoon grated

Fresh lemon juice, 1 tablespoon

Large or extra-large eggs, 8

Unsalted butter, 4–6 tablespoons

Brioche, 8 slices, each about 1 inch thick

Confectioners' sugar, ¼ cup

To make the apple chutney, in a nonaluminum saucepan, combine the apples, raisins, figs, brown sugar, wine, lemon zest, and lemon juice. Place over medium heat and warm, stirring, until the sugar dissolves. Reduce the heat to very low, cover, and cook, stirring occasionally, until the apples can be easily pierced with a fork, about 40 minutes. Remove from the heat and set aside to cool to room temperature. (The chutney can be made up to 2 weeks in advance. Let cool completely, then cover tightly and refrigerate.)

Break the eggs into a shallow bowl and beat with a fork until the whites and yolks are blended. In a large frying pan over medium heat, melt 2 tablespoons of the butter. When the butter foams, immerse the brioche slices, one at a time, in the beaten eggs and then place them in the hot pan, adding only as many as will fit without crowding. Cook until golden brown on the bottom, about 4 minutes. Turn them over with a spatula and cook until the other side is golden, about 4 minutes more. Transfer the toasts to a warmed platter and cover with aluminum foil to keep warm. Repeat with the remaining brioche slices, adding more butter as needed to prevent sticking.

Sift the confectioners' sugar evenly over the French toasts. Serve right away, accompanied by the apple chutney.

SERVES 4

Ricotta & Banana Pancakes

Adding ricotta cheese to pancake batter gives the pancakes a light texture, as does beating the egg whites separately before folding them into the batter. In addition to the sweet banana topping, you can serve these pancakes with pure maple syrup.

To make the spiced bananas, in a small bowl, combine the flour, sugar, cinnamon, and nutmeg. Dredge the bananas in the mixture and shake off the excess. In a frying pan over medium-high heat, melt the butter. When the butter foams, add the coated bananas and fry until crisp, about 5 minutes. Transfer to paper towels to drain.

In a large bowl, whisk together the flour, baking powder, and salt. In another bowl, whisk together the yolks, ricotta, and milk. Stir the egg mixture into the flour mixture just until blended. In a bowl, using a handheld electric mixer, beat the egg whites and sugar until stiff peaks form, about 2 minutes. Using a rubber spatula, gently fold the whites into the ricotta mixture until incorporated.

Heat a griddle over medium-high heat. Add 2 teaspoons butter. When the butter foams, pour 2 tablespoons of batter onto the griddle into rounds about 3 inches in diameter and spaced 1 inch apart. Cook until the batter bubbles and the bottoms are golden, 1–2 minutes. Turn over the pancakes with a spatula and cook the other side until golden, 1–2 minutes more. Transfer the pancakes to a warmed platter and cover with aluminum foil to keep warm. Cook the remaining batter, adding more butter to the griddle as needed. Spoon the spiced bananas over the top of the pancakes and serve warm.

MAKES ABOUT 24 SMALL PANCAKES; SERVES 6–8

SPICED BANANAS

All-purpose flour, 2 tablespoons

Sugar, 1 tablespoon

Ground cinnamon, ½ teaspoon

Nutmeg, ¼ teaspoon freshly grated

Firm bananas, 2, cut into ½-inch pieces

Unsalted butter, 1 tablespoon

All-purpose flour, 1 cup

Baking powder, 1 tablespoon

Salt, ¼ teaspoon

Large or extra-large eggs, 2, separated

Whole-milk ricotta cheese, 1 cup

Whole milk, ⅔ cup

Sugar, 2 tablespoons

Unsalted butter for cooking

Brown-Sugar Coffee Cake

This classic coffee cake owes its extra-moist texture to the sour cream in the batter. Serve it as part of a brunch buffet, as a sweet foil to Spring Vegetable Frittata (page 35), or to complement Fresh Berry Salad with Mint (page 22).

All-purpose flour, 1½ cups

Granulated sugar, ½ cup

Baking powder, 2 teaspoons

Salt, ½ teaspoon

Large or extra-large egg, 1

Sour cream, ½ cup

Whole milk, ¼ cup

Unsalted butter, 4 tablespoons, melted and slightly cooled

Granny Smith apple, 1, peeled, cored, and chopped (about 1 cup)

TOPPING

Light brown sugar, ½ cup firmly packed

All-purpose flour, ¼ cup

Cold unsalted butter, 3 tablespoons, cut into ½-inch pieces

Chopped walnuts, ½ cup

Preheat the oven to 400°F. Butter an 8-inch square baking pan.

In a large bowl, whisk together the flour, granulated sugar, baking powder, and salt. In a medium bowl, whisk the egg just until the yolk and white are blended. Add the sour cream, milk, and melted butter and mix well. Pour the egg mixture into the flour mixture and stir just until the ingredients are blended. Stir in the chopped apple. Spread the batter evenly in the prepared baking pan.

To make the topping, in a bowl, combine the brown sugar, flour, and butter. Using your fingertips, work the ingredients together until a coarse, crumbly mixture forms. Add the walnuts and mix well with your fingertips. Sprinkle the topping evenly over the batter.

Bake the coffee cake until the topping is browned and a sharp knife inserted into the center comes out clean, about 30 minutes. Let cool for about 5 minutes, then cut into squares and serve warm or at room temperature.

SERVES 6–8

Orange-Zest Scones

Orange zest lends its tangy flavor to these simple scones. Serve them with lemon curd to reinforce the fresh citrus flavor. They are a delicious accompaniment to Herbed Pork Sausages (page 103) and can easily be paired with any style of eggs.

All-purpose flour, 2½ cups

Light brown sugar, ½ cup firmly packed

Baking powder, 2 teaspoons

Baking soda, 1 teaspoon

Salt, 1 teaspoon

Orange zest, ¼ cup coarsely grated

Cold unsalted butter, 6 tablespoons, cut into ½-inch pieces

Whole milk, ½ cup plus 1 tablespoon

Large egg, 1, lightly beaten

Fresh orange juice, 3 tablespoons

Golden raisins, ¼ cup

Purchased lemon curd, 1 cup for serving

Preheat the oven to 400°F. Lightly butter a rimmed baking sheet.

In a food processor, combine the flour, brown sugar, baking powder, baking soda, salt, and orange zest and pulse to mix the ingredients. Add the butter and pulse just until the mixture is the consistency of coarse meal, 4–5 times. Then, add the milk, egg, and orange juice and process just until the mixture holds together, about 20 seconds. Transfer the dough to a bowl and stir in the golden raisins.

Turn the dough out onto a lightly floured work surface and gently knead into a ball. Using a floured rolling pin, roll out the dough to about ½ inch thick. Flour a 3-inch round biscuit cutter and use it to cut out as many rounds as possible, placing them on the prepared baking sheet. Gather the scraps, press them together, roll them out, cut out more rounds, and add them to the baking sheet. (You should have about 12 rounds total.)

Bake until the scones are golden brown, about 15 minutes. Transfer them to a wire rack and let cool for 15 minutes. Spoon the lemon curd into a small bowl. Serve the scones warm, with the lemon curd.

MAKES 12 SCONES; SERVES 6

Oatmeal-Blueberry Muffins

Toasting the oatmeal brings out its flavor and adds a subtle nutty taste to these muffins. Frozen or fresh blueberries can be used, making this a good year-round recipe. For the best results, be careful not to break the berries when you add them to the batter.

Preheat the oven to 425°F. Line a 12-cup muffin tin with paper or silicone liners.

In a frying pan over medium heat, toast the oats, stirring constantly with a wooden spoon, until they are fragrant and show just a hint of gold, 4–5 minutes. Remove from the heat and let cool slightly.

In a bowl, whisk together the toasted oats, flour, sugar, baking powder, baking soda, and salt. Add the buttermilk, egg, and melted butter and mix with a wooden spoon until the dry ingredients are moistened. Gently stir in the blueberries.

Divide the batter among the prepared muffin cups, filling them nearly to the brim. Bake the muffins until they are puffed and lightly browned, 20–25 minutes. Let cool in the pan for 10 minutes, then turn out onto a rack. Serve warm or at room temperature.

MAKES 12 MUFFINS; SERVES 6

Quick-cooking rolled oats, 1¼ cups

All-purpose flour, 1 cup

Sugar, ⅓ cup

Baking powder, 1 teaspoon

Baking soda, ½ teaspoon

Salt, ½ teaspoon

Buttermilk, 1 cup

Large or extra-large egg, 1

Unsalted butter, 4 tablespoons, melted and slightly cooled

Fresh or frozen blueberries, 1 cup

Blackberry Blintzes

Blintzes, cousins to French crêpes, are thin, pliable pancakes that are filled with fruit or cheese, folded or rolled, and then baked or briefly fried before serving. This version features a sweet blackberry filling with a rich sour cream topping.

Preheat the oven to 375°F. Butter 1 large or 2 small baking dish(es) large enough to hold the rolled pancakes in a single layer.

In a saucepan over medium heat, combine the blackberries and granulated sugar. Heat, stirring constantly, until the sugar dissolves and the berries are warmed through, 4–5 minutes. The berries should still be whole. Remove from the heat.

To fill the blintzes, place 1 pancake on a work surface. Spoon about 2 tablespoons of the berry mixture in the center of a pancake. Fold the edge nearest you over the filling, then fold in the sides and roll up the pancake into a compact cylinder. Place the filled blintz seam side down in the prepared baking dish. Repeat until all of the blintzes have been filled. Drizzle the filled blintzes with the melted butter.

Bake the blintzes until lightly golden and hot all the way through, about 20 minutes. Remove from the oven and let the pan cool on a wire rack for about 5 minutes.

Using a fine-mesh sieve, sift confectioners' sugar lightly over the blintzes, and pour any leftover filling over the top. Serve warm and pass the sour cream in a bowl at the table.

MAKES 8 BLINTZES; SERVES 4

Blackberries, 1 pound (about 2 pints)

Granulated sugar, ½ cup

Blintz-Style Pancakes (page 68), 8

Unsalted butter, 3 tablespoons, melted

Confectioners' sugar for serving

Sour cream for serving

Blintz-Style Pancakes

These thin pancakes are light but sturdy, so they can be stuffed with flavorful fillings and then baked. Use them to make Blackberry Blintzes (page 67) or fill them with the fruit or cheese mixture of your choice, roll them tightly, and bake them as directed.

All-purpose flour, 1 cup

Salt, 1/2 teaspoon

Whole milk, 1 1/4 cups

Water, 1/2 cup

Large egg, 1

Unsalted butter, 1 tablespoon, melted, plus 4 teaspoons for cooking

In a large bowl, whisk together the flour and salt. Add the milk and water and whisk until blended and no lumps remain. Beat in the egg and the 1 tablespoon melted butter until smooth and lump free.

Heat a 7- or 8-inch frying pan, preferably nonstick, over medium-high heat. When it is hot, add 1/2 teaspoon of the butter. Tilt the pan from side to side to coat the bottom with the butter as it melts. Pour about 1/4 cup of the batter into the pan, quickly tilting and swirling the pan to coat the bottom with the batter. Let the pancake cook until the edges brown and begin to curl and pull away from the pan, 1–2 minutes. Using tongs, turn the pancake over and cook the other side just until lightly golden, 20–30 seconds more. It should not brown. Transfer the pancake to a platter and cover with aluminum foil to keep warm. Repeat until all of the batter has been used, adding 1/2 teaspoon butter to the pan before cooking each pancake. (You should have about 8 pancakes.)

MAKES 8 PANCAKES; SERVES 4

Jam-Filled Sweet Crêpes

Crêpes, the thin, delicate pancakes beloved of French cooking, make a wonderful brunch dish. For easy and tasty fillings, provide bowls of assorted jams. A selection of soft cheeses, such as ricotta, cream, or farmer cheese, can be offered as well.

In a large bowl, whisk the eggs with the 1¾ cups milk. Slowly add the flour, sugar, and salt, whisking constantly to avoid lumps. Cover and refrigerate for 2 hours. When ready to cook, stir the batter well. It should be the consistency of heavy cream. If it is too thick, thin with a little more milk.

Heat a 12-inch nonstick frying pan over medium-high heat. When it is hot, add about 1 teaspoon of the butter. Tilt the pan from side to side to coat the bottom with the butter as it melts. Pour about ¼ cup of the batter into the pan, quickly tilting and swirling the pan to coat the bottom with the batter. Pour any excess batter back into the bowl and put the pan back on the heat. Let the crêpe cook until its center bubbles and the edges begin to dry, about 30 seconds. Using tongs, turn the crêpe over and cook the other side until golden, about 20 seconds more. Transfer the crêpe to a plate and cover with aluminum foil to keep warm. Repeat with the remaining butter and crêpe batter, adding about 1 teaspoon of butter to the pan before cooking each crêpe. (You should have 16 crêpes total.)

To serve, put the jams in small bowls and set them on the table with individual spreaders. Invite your guests to take 2–4 crêpes, fill them with the jam(s) of choice, and fold or roll the crêpes over the jam.

MAKES 16 CRÊPES; SERVES 4–8

Large or extra-large eggs, 4

Whole milk, 1¾ cups plus more as needed for thinning

All-purpose flour, ⅓ cup

Sugar, 2 tablespoons

Salt, ½ teaspoon

Unsalted butter, about 5 tablespoons for cooking

Assorted jams such as blackberry, cherry, plum, and strawberry for serving

main dishes

Tips for Brewing Great Coffee

Beloved by coffee afficionados, a French press coffee pot will produce deep, rich, fresh coffee, a few cups at a time. For the best flavor, always use freshly ground coffee beans.

Warm the pot by pouring some boiling spring water into it, swirling the water, letting it sit for a minute, and then pouring it out.

Measure coarsely ground coffee into the pot, allowing 2 tablespoons per cup. Pour in ¾ cup just-boiled spring water per cup. Place the lid on the pot with the strainer just touching the top of the water.

Let the coffee steep for 4–6 minutes, depending on how strong you prefer your brew. Then, slowly push down the strainer as far as it will go to trap the grounds.

Serve the coffee right away. Set milk or half-and-half and sugar on the table for your guests.

Steak & Eggs

This classic brunch offering is dressed up with the addition of warm Caramelized Onions (page 76). Sautéed Cherry Tomatoes (page 93), Roasted Rosemary Potatoes (page 96), and Sweet Polenta with Pecans (page 97) also make great accompaniments.

In a large frying pan over medium-high heat, melt the butter. When it foams, add the steaks and sprinkle with 1 teaspoon of the salt and ¾ teaspoon of the pepper. Cook until the steaks are browned on the bottom, about 4 minutes. Using a spatula or tongs, turn over the steaks and sprinkle with the remaining 1 teaspoon salt and ¾ teaspoon pepper. Cook the steaks until done to your liking, 3–4 minutes more for medium-rare, or 5–6 minutes more for medium. Transfer the steaks to a warmed platter, reserving the juices in the pan, and cover with aluminum foil to keep warm.

Return the pan to medium heat and warm the pan juices. When they are hot, crack the eggs into the pan and fry the eggs sunny-side up or over easy as directed on page 42.

Divide the steaks among warmed individual plates. Top each steak with a portion of Caramelized Onions and serve right away, with a fried egg alongside.

SERVES 4

Unsalted butter, 1½ tablespoons

Boneless rib-eye or other steaks, 4, each about ½ inch thick

Sea salt or kosher salt, 2 teaspoons

Freshly ground pepper, 1½ teaspoons

Large or extra-large eggs, 4

Caramelized Onions (page 76)

Caramelized Onions

This method of cooking onions brings out their natural sugars, mellowing their usually sharp flavor. These can be made up to two days in advance. Let them cool completely, cover them tightly, and store them in the refrigerator. Reheat them gently just before using.

Unsalted butter,
1 tablespoon

Extra-virgin olive oil,
1 tablespoon

Yellow onions,
1½ pounds, very thinly sliced on a mandolin or with a knife

Fresh thyme leaves,
1 teaspoon

Sea salt or kosher salt,
½ teaspoon

Water, dry white wine, or beef broth,
2 tablespoons

In a large frying pan over medium heat, melt the butter with the olive oil. When the butter foams, add the onions, thyme, and salt and stir well. Reduce the heat to very low, cover, and cook until the onions soften and release their juices, 25–30 minutes. Uncover and stir well. Increase the heat to medium and continue to cook, stirring frequently, until the onions are golden brown and caramelized, about 10 minutes more.

Add the water and scrape up any browned bits from the bottom of the pan. Remove from the heat and serve warm.

MAKES 1–2 CUPS

Red Flannel Hash

Red flannel hash is so-called because beets are added to the typical mixture of boiled potatoes, corned beef, and onions, turning the dish a distinctive red color. A classic way to serve hash at brunch is to top it with one or two Poached Eggs (page 38).

Place the beets in a saucepan, cover with water by 2 inches, and bring to a boil over high heat. Reduce the heat to medium, cover, and cook until the beets can be pierced with a fork, about 1 hour. Meanwhile, in another saucepan, cover the potatoes with water by 2 inches and bring to a boil over high heat. Reduce the heat to medium, cover, and cook until the potatoes can be pierced with a fork, 35–40 minutes.

Drain the cooked beets and potatoes and let both cool. Peel the cooled beets and potatoes and then cut them into ¼-inch cubes.

In a bowl, stir together the potatoes, beets, and corned beef. In a large frying pan over medium-high heat, warm the oil. Add the onion and sauté until translucent, 2–3 minutes. Layer the corned beef mixture on top of the onion and press flat with a metal spatula. Sprinkle with the salt to taste and the pepper. Cook, without turning, until a brown crust has formed on the bottom and the edges pull away from the sides of the pan, about 20 minutes.

Remove from the heat and invert a large, flat platter on top. Using pot holders, hold both the frying pan and the platter firmly and invert them together. Lift off the frying pan, exposing the crusty bottom of the hash. Sprinkle with the parsley, cut into wedges, and serve.

SERVES 4

Beets, 2, stems trimmed down to 1 inch

Red or white boiling potatoes, 3, of uniform size (about 1 pound)

Corned beef, 1 pound, cut into ½-inch cubes

Corn, canola, or other vegetable oil, 2 tablespoons

Yellow onion, 1 small, chopped

Sea salt or kosher salt, ¼–½ teaspoon

Freshly ground pepper, ½ teaspoon

Fresh flat-leaf parsley, ¼ cup chopped

Turkey & Yukon Gold Hash

Here, ground turkey makes a lighter version of a classic brunch dish. Serve it with cornbread wedges, Poached Eggs (page 38), or turn it into a scramble by adding four or five beaten eggs and skipping the extra cooking that creates the crust.

Yukon gold potatoes, 1 pound, of uniform size

Sea salt or kosher salt, 3 teaspoons

Grapeseed, canola, or other vegetable oil, about 3 tablespoons

Ground turkey, 1 pound

Fresh sage, 2 tablespoons chopped

Freshly ground pepper, ½ teaspoon

Green bell pepper, 1, seeded and finely chopped

Yellow onion, ⅔ cup chopped

Place the potatoes in a saucepan, cover with water by 2 inches, add 2 teaspoons of the salt, and bring to a boil over high heat. Reduce the heat to medium, cover, and cook until the potatoes can be easily pierced with a fork, 35–40 minutes. Drain, let cool, then peel and cut the potatoes into ¼-inch cubes.

In a frying pan over high heat, warm 1 tablespoon of the oil. Add the ground turkey, sage, ½ teaspoon of the salt, and ¼ teaspoon of the pepper. Sauté until browned, 7–8 minutes. Transfer the turkey to paper towels to drain. Leave the fat in the pan.

In a bowl, combine the turkey, potatoes, and bell pepper. Add oil to the pan to total 2 tablespoons fat and oil and warm over medium-high heat. Add the onion and sauté until softened, 2–3 minutes. Layer the turkey mixture on top of the onion and press flat with a metal spatula. Add the remaining salt and pepper. Cook, without turning, until a brown crust forms on the bottom, 15–20 minutes.

Remove from the heat and invert a large, flat platter on top. Using pot holders, hold both the frying pan and the platter firmly and invert them together. Lift off the frying pan, exposing the crusty bottom of the hash. Sprinkle with the parsley, cut into wedges, and serve.

SERVES 4

Chicken & Fontina Panini

Sandwiches grilled in a pan or a panini press make a satisfying brunch dish, and can be easily varied to offer guests different selections. Try panini with sliced ham or turkey, roasted bell peppers or eggplant, and Gruyère, goat, or blue cheese.

Preheat a panini press according to the manufacturer's directions, or heat a large nonstick frying pan over medium-high heat. Meanwhile, cut each focaccia square in half horizontally and place the bottoms and tops cut side up on a work surface. In a small bowl, combine the mayonnaise and mustard. Spread the cut surface of each focaccia square with the mayonnaise mixture. Layer the sliced chicken breasts, arugula leaves, and cheese on the bottom halves, dividing the ingredients evenly, then put the remaining focaccia pieces on top, spread-side down.

Brush the panini press or frying pan with 1 teaspoon olive oil. Place the sandwiches in the press or pan and brush the tops with another 1 teaspoon of the olive oil. If using a panini press, close the machine and cook until the bread shows golden grid marks, 3–5 minutes. (If using a frying pan, flatten the sandwiches slightly with a spatula, and then cook until the bottom is golden brown, about 5 minutes. Turn the sandwiches over, press down again with the spatula, and then cook until the other side is golden, 3–4 minutes more.)

To serve, cut each sandwich in half on the diagonal and place on warmed individual plates. Serve warm, with extra sauce on the side, if desired.

MAKES 4 SANDWICHES; SERVES 4

Focaccia, 4 pieces, each 4 inches square

Mayonnaise, 1/4 cup

Dijon mustard, 2 teaspoons

Poached Chicken Breasts (page 82), 2, cut into thin slices

Arugula leaves, 1 cup

Fontina cheese, 1/4 pound, thinly sliced

Extra-virgin olive oil, 2–4 teaspoons

Poached Chicken Breasts

These flavorful, moist chicken breasts are a brunch staple. They can be used to make Chicken & Fontina Panini (page 81), in egg scrambles, or as a filling for omelettes. Cooking them with their bones and skin intact ensures that the meat stays juicy.

Bone-in, skin-on chicken breasts,
2 (about ⅔ pound)

Sea salt or kosher salt,
1 teaspoon

Freshly ground pepper,
1 teaspoon

Extra-virgin olive oil,
2 teaspoons

Fresh sage, 2 teaspoons minced

Dry white wine, ¼ cup

Season the chicken breasts all over with the salt and pepper. In a deep sauté pan over medium-high heat, warm the 2 teaspoons olive oil. When the oil is hot, add the chicken breasts, skin side down, and sprinkle with the sage. Cook until the skin is golden, 4–5 minutes. Turn the breasts over and cook the other side until lightly golden, 3–4 minutes more.

Add the wine and stir to scrape up the browned bits clinging to the pan bottom. Add water to cover the chicken breasts by ½ inch, cover the pan, reduce the heat to low, and simmer gently until the chicken is opaque throughout, about 20 minutes. Using a slotted spoon, transfer the chicken to a colander to cool and discard the poaching liquid. (The chicken can be made up to 1 day in advance. Let cool completely, then cover tightly and refrigerate.)

Pull off the skin from the chicken breasts and discard. Use your fingers to pull all the meat from the bones in a single piece and discard the bones. Use as desired.

MAKES 2

Sausage & Cheddar Strata

Strata, Italian-style bread pudding, makes a hearty one-dish meal that needs only fruit or a salad to complete the menu. For a variation, use one-half pound of bacon instead of sausage, and one-quarter pound of Gorgonzola for the Cheddar.

In a frying pan over medium heat, sauté the sausages, turning occasionally, until golden brown on all sides, 5–6 minutes for fully cooked sausages and 12–15 minutes for uncooked sausages. Remove from the heat and transfer to a cutting board. Let the sausages cool, then cut into slices ½ inch thick.

Butter a deep 2½-quart baking dish. Arrange one-third of the bread slices on the bottom of the prepared dish, cutting the slices if needed to fill any gaps. Top with one-third of the sausages, and then with one-third of the cheese. Repeat the layering 2 more times, ending with cheese. Break the eggs into a bowl, pour in the milk, and whisk until well blended. Pour the egg mixture into the baking dish, being careful not to dislodge the layers. Cover and refrigerate for at least 1 hour or for up to 24 hours before baking.

Preheat the oven to 350°F. Cover the strata with aluminum foil and bake for 45 minutes. Remove the foil and continue to bake until the top is golden brown and a knife inserted into the center comes out clean, about 15 minutes more. Transfer the baking dish to a wire rack, cover loosely with aluminum foil, and let cool for about 10 minutes.

Scoop the strata onto warmed plates and serve right away.

SERVES 4–6

Sausages, such as mild Italian, chicken and fennel, or andouille, 3 links (about 3 pounds)

Day-old baguette, ciabatta, or other country-style bread, 15 slices, each about 2 inches in diameter and ½ inch thick

Cheddar cheese, ¼ pound, coarsely shredded

Large or extra-large eggs, 3

Whole milk, 1½ cups

Breakfast Pizzas

Popular in France and Italy, these egg-topped pizzas will be a conversation starter at the brunch table. They should be served as soon as they are baked, making them the perfect choice for a casual brunch centered around the kitchen island.

Bulk pork or chicken sausage, 1 pound

Cornmeal for cooking the pizzas

Pizza Dough (page 86), rolled into six 8-inch rounds

Olive oil for brushing

Feta cheese, 6 ounces, crumbled

Large or extra-large eggs, 6

Sea salt or kosher salt

Freshly ground pepper

Green onion, 4, with 2 inches of tender green tops, minced

Preheat the oven to 450°F.

Warm a frying pan over medium-high heat. Add the sausage and sauté, breaking up the meat with a wooden spoon, until the pieces are about the size of walnuts and show only a hint of pink, about 7–8 minutes. Using a slotted spoon, transfer the sausage to paper towels to drain.

Dust a rimless baking sheet with cornmeal and place a dough round on it. Top the dough round with one-sixth each of the sausage and cheese, leaving an area in the center uncovered to put the egg. Brush the crust edges with oil.

Crack an egg onto the uncovered center of the pizza round and sprinkle with salt and pepper to taste. Place the baking sheet on the middle rack of the oven. Bake until the crust is crisp and golden, the cheese is melted, and the egg is fully cooked, about 12 minutes.

Remove the pizza from the oven and, using 2 spatulas, carefully transfer it to a plate. Top with the green onions.

Serve the pizza right away. Repeat until all of the dough rounds have been topped and baked.

MAKES SIX 8-INCH PIZZAS; SERVES 6–12

Pizza Dough

This pizza dough is perfect for Breakfast Pizzas (page 84), but it is versatile and can be tailored to complement any brunch menu. Top it with your favorite combination of sauce, cheese, vegetables, and meat and bake each round as directed.

Active dry yeast, 1 envelope

Warm water, 1½ cups

Extra-virgin olive oil, 2 tablespoons

Semolina flour, ½ cup

Salt, 1 tablespoon

All-purpose flour, 3–4 cups, plus extra for dusting

In the bowl of a stand mixer, sprinkle the dry yeast over the warm water and let stand until foamy, about 4 minutes. Place the bowl on the mixer fitted with the dough hook and add the olive oil, semolina flour, and salt; mix until combined. Add the all-purpose flour, ½ cup at a time, and knead with the dough hook until the dough is smooth but not sticky, about 10 minutes.

Form the dough into a ball, put in a lightly oiled bowl, and turn to coat with oil. Cover the bowl with a clean kitchen towel and let rise in a warm, draft-free place until doubled in bulk, about 1 hour.

Punch down the dough, transfer to a lightly floured work surface, and divide equally into 6 balls, kneading the balls briefly as you shape them. Cover with the towel and let rise until doubled in bulk, about 45 minutes. Working with 1 ball of dough at a time, flatten and gently stretch or roll out into a round about 8 inches in diameter.

Top, bake, and use the pizza dough as desired.

MAKES SIX 8-INCH DOUGH ROUNDS

Croque-Monsieur

This French favorite is essentially a ham sandwich covered with bubbling-hot cheese sauce. It is perfect at a casual brunch, paired with a green salad. To make croque-madames, top each sandwich with a Fried Egg (page 42) before adding the sauce.

Butter one side of each slice of bread. Lay 2 slices of ham on the unbuttered side of one slice, then top with a second slice, buttered-side up. Repeat with the remaining ham and bread.

To make the sauce, in a saucepan over medium heat, melt the butter. Remove the pan from the heat and whisk in the flour, salt, and pepper. Return the pan to medium heat and slowly whisk the milk. Reduce the heat to low and cook, stirring, until the sauce thickens, about 15 minutes. Stir in $1/4$ cup of the cheese and remove from the heat.

Position a rack about 6 inches from the heat source, and preheat the broiler. Line the rack of a broiler pan with aluminum foil.

Meanwhile, warm a large frying pan over medium heat. When it is hot, place the sandwiches in the pan and cook until the bottoms are golden, about 4 minutes. Turn over the sandwiches and cook until the other sides are golden, about 4 minutes more.

Transfer the sandwiches to the broiler pan and pour about $1/4$ cup of the cheese sauce over each sandwich. Top the sandwiches with the remaining $1/2$ cup cheese, dividing it evenly. Broil the sandwiches until the sauce bubbles and the cheese is golden, 4–5 minutes. Remove from the broiler, transfer to warmed plates, and serve right away.

MAKES 4 SANDWICHES

Unsalted butter, 2 tablespoons at room temperature

Brioche or sandwich bread, 8 slices

Ham, 8 thin slices

CHEESE SAUCE

Unsalted butter, 2 tablespoons

All-purpose flour, 2 tablespoons

Sea salt or kosher salt, 1½ teaspoons

Cayenne pepper, ⅛ teaspoon

Whole milk, 1½ cups

Gruyère cheese, ¾ cup shredded

side dishes

Tips for Setting Up a Brunch Buffet

Brunch buffets should convey abundance. Choose a table that is just large enough to hold everything and select food that is easy to eat from a plate balanced on the knees.

Drape a sideboard or counter with a colorful tablecloth; bundle the flatware in complementary napkins.

Determine the traffic flow, then set plates and bowls at the beginning of the buffet and the flatware at the end. This will help guests move easily along the buffet.

Arrange the food in the order in which it will be eaten. Serve some of the items on pedestals or in footed bowls to create an attractive look and to facilitate serving.

Adorn the buffet with a flower arrangement or other accessories, if desired, provided they do not interfere with serving. Remember to put out appropriate serving utensils for each dish.

Sautéed Cherry Tomatoes

Cherry tomatoes require just a few minutes of cooking to warm them through. Here, they are accented by aromatic fresh basil leaves. Serve this easy side dish alongside Steak & Eggs (page 75) or Sausage & Cheddar Strata (page 83).

In a large frying pan over medium-high heat, warm the olive oil. When hot, add the tomatoes and cook, stirring constantly with a wooden spoon, until shiny and some of the skins just begin to burst, 4–5 minutes. Sprinkle with the salt and transfer to a serving bowl.

Add the basil leaves, and turn several times. Serve hot, warm, or at room temperature.

SERVES 4–6

Extra-virgin olive oil,
3 tablespoons

Cherry tomatoes,
3 cups, preferably a mixture of colors and shapes, stems removed

Sea salt or kosher salt,
½ teaspoon

Fresh basil leaves,
½ cup, preferably a mixture of purple and green varieties

Roasted Spiced Apples

Apples stuffed with sugar and nuts are a flavorful accompaniment to dishes that include bacon, ham, or sausage. Select a good cooking apple—one that holds its shape in the intense heat of the oven—such as Granny Smith, Gala, or Golden Delicious.

Large, firm cooking apples, 6

Dark brown sugar, ¾ cup firmly packed

Chopped pecans, ½ cup

Lemon zest, 4 teaspoons finely grated

Nutmeg, 1½ teaspoons freshly grated

Ground cardamom, ½ teaspoon

Pure maple syrup, 3 tablespoons

Unsalted butter, 2 tablespoons, cut into 6 pieces

Cinnamon sticks, 6, each 4–5 inches long

Preheat the oven to 350°F. Using a circular apple corer, remove the core from the apples, stopping ½ inch from the bottom. Set aside.

In a small bowl, using a large spoon, stir together the brown sugar, pecans, lemon zest, nutmeg, and cardamom. Add the maple syrup and mix well. Using a small spoon, pack the center of each apple with one-sixth of the mixture. Dot the top of each apple with one-sixth of the butter.

Carefully place the apples in a baking dish just large enough to hold them snugly. Insert a cinnamon stick into the stuffed core of each apple, pushing it down as far as it will go. Add water to a depth of ¼ inch to the baking dish.

Roast the apples, using a spoon to baste them several times with their juices, until the skins shrivel and the flesh can be easily pierced with a fork, 45 minutes.

Let cool for 5 minutes, then serve warm, directly from the baking dish.

SERVES 6

Roasted Rosemary Potatoes

If you can't find small red potatoes, cut larger ones into 2-inch pieces. You can substitute 2 tablespoons of sage or thyme for the rosemary. For an old-fashioned meal, serve these potatoes with Herbed Pork Sausages (page 103), Fried Eggs (page 42), and toast.

Small red potatoes,
1½ pounds, each about
1 inch in diameter,
unpeeled

Extra-virgin olive oil,
2 tablespoons

Sea salt or kosher salt,
2–3 teaspoons

Freshly ground pepper,
1 teaspoon

Fresh rosemary,
2 tablespoons minced

Preheat the oven to 350°F. Place the potatoes in a shallow baking dish just large enough to hold them snugly in a single layer. Drizzle the potatoes with the olive oil and, using a wooden spoon, turn to coat them well with the oil. Sprinkle with the salt to taste, the pepper, and the rosemary, and turn again to coat.

Roast the potatoes, turning once or twice, until the skin wrinkles and the potatoes can be easily pierced with a fork, about 1¼ hours.

Transfer the potatoes to a warmed, shallow serving bowl and serve hot or at room temperature.

SERVES 4–6

Sweet Polenta with Pecans

Serve this comforting, cool-weather dish with Herbed Pork Sausages (page 103) or Crispy Pepper Bacon (page 102) for a complete meal. Any leftover polenta can be chilled, then sliced and fried and served with another dish, such as Piperade & Poached Eggs (page 36).

Preheat the oven to 300°F. Spread the pecans in a single layer on a rimmed baking sheet. Toast in the oven, stirring once or twice, until they take on color and are fragrant, about 10 minutes. Transfer to a plate and let cool completely, then coarsely chop and set aside. (The nuts can be toasted and chopped up to 3 days in advance and stored in an airtight container at room temperature.)

In a saucepan, bring the water to a boil over high heat and add the salt. Slowly pour in the polenta in a steady stream, stirring constantly with a wooden spoon. Reduce the heat to low and cook, stirring frequently, until the water is absorbed and the polenta has thickened and pulls away from the sides of the pan, about 40 minutes. Remove from the heat and stir in the butter and mascarpone.

Transfer the polenta to a warmed serving bowl, drizzle with the maple syrup, and garnish with the toasted pecans. Serve right away.

SERVES 4

Pecans, ½ cup

Water, 6 cups

Salt, 1 tablespoon

Polenta, 1 cup

Unsalted butter, 1 tablespoon

Mascarpone cheese, ½ cup

Pure maple syrup, 1–2 teaspoons

Savory Bread Pudding

The texture of this pudding will be either chewy or soft, depending on the type of bread you prefer to use. Coarse-crumbed country-style bread makes a sturdier pudding, while fine-crumbed sandwich bread yields a softer version.

Preheat the oven to 350°F. Butter a 3-quart soufflé dish.

Place the bread slices in a shallow bowl and pour in 2 cups of the milk. Let the bread soak up the liquid, 5–10 minutes. (If the bread is very dry, it will take longer and may require up to 1/2 cup more milk.) Remove the bread, squeeze out any excess milk with your hands, and put the bread in a clean bowl. Discard the milk.

In another bowl, combine the eggs, salt, pepper, and the remaining 1/2 cup milk and whisk to blend. Layer one-third of the bread in the prepared dish. Top with one-third of the Gruyère cheese and half of the herbs. Repeat the layers, reserving 1 tablespoon of the herbs. Arrange the last third of the bread on top and sprinkle with the remaining Gruyère cheese and the Romano cheese. Pour the egg mixture evenly over the top. Use a knife to push the bread away from the sides of dish, letting the egg mixture run to the bottom. Dot the top of the bread pudding with the butter.

Bake the bread pudding until the top is crusty and golden and a knife inserted into the center comes out clean, 45–60 minutes. Garnish with the reserved herbs, scoop the pudding onto warmed individual plates, and serve right away.

SERVES 6–8

Dry country-style bread or sandwich bread, 12–16 slices

Whole milk, 2 1/2–3 cups

Large or extra-large eggs, 5

Sea salt or kosher salt, 1 teaspoon

Freshly ground pepper, 1 teaspoon

Gruyère cheese, 1/2 pound, coarsely shredded

Mixed fresh herbs, such as flat-leaf parsley, chives, and tarragon, 1/2 cup chopped

Romano cheese, 1/4 cup freshly grated

Unsalted butter, 1 tablespoon, cut into pieces

Potato Pancakes

The trick to making crisp pancakes is to use potatoes with a very high starch content and to squeeze out all of their excess moisture before you fry them. Serve these with any egg dish or as a classic accompaniment to a Lox & Bagel Bar (page 27).

Russet potatoes,
1½–2 pounds, peeled

Extra-large eggs,
2, lightly beaten

All-purpose flour,
1½ tablespoons

Yellow onion,
1 tablespoon grated

Sea salt or kosher salt,
¾ teaspoon

Grapeseed or canola oil, or unsalted butter,
¼–½ cup

Sea salt or kosher salt,
1 teaspoon

Crème fraîche, ½ cup
for serving

Using the large holes on a box grater-shredder, coarsely shred the potatoes into a bowl. Using your hands, squeeze out as much moisture as possible from the potatoes, then place them in a clean bowl. Add the eggs, flour, onion, and salt to the potatoes and mix well with a wooden spoon.

In a frying pan over medium-high heat, warm the oil. Working in batches, drop tablespoonfuls of the potato mixture into the hot oil, spaced about 2 inches apart, and flatten each into a 3-inch round with a metal spatula. Cook until the pancakes are golden brown on the bottom, 1–2 minutes. Using the spatula, turn the pancakes over and cook until the other side is golden brown and the pancakes are cooked through, 1–2 minutes more. Do not let them burn. Transfer the pancakes to paper towels to drain, then transfer to a warmed platter and cover with aluminum foil to keep warm. Repeat to cook the remaining potato mixture, adding more oil as needed.

Sprinkle the pancakes with the sea salt. Serve warm, accompanied by the crème fraîche.

MAKES ABOUT TEN 3-INCH PANCAKES; SERVES 4

Crispy Pepper Bacon

Although bacon comes with many cures and flavors, it is easy to flavor your own with a little freshly ground black pepper. Experiment with different kinds of peppercorns, such as Aleppo, Tellicherry, or Malabar, to make the flavor even more distinctive.

Applewood–smoked bacon, 8 thick slices

Coarse freshly ground pepper, 1 tablespoon

Preheat the broiler and position an oven rack about 8 inches from the heat source. Line the lower part of a broiler pan with aluminum foil and put the upper rack in place.

Lay the bacon slices on a work surface. Rub the pepper evenly over one side of the bacon slices, pressing with your fingertips to make sure the pepper adheres. (The bacon can be seasoned up to 24 hours in advance, tightly wrapped, and stored in the refrigerator.)

Lay the bacon on the broiler pan. Broil, turning once, until the bacon is crispy, about 8 minutes total. Serve right away.

SERVES 4

Herbed Pork Sausages

It's easy to prepare your own sausage patties by adding fresh herbs and other seasonings to ground pork. You can use a dry pan when you fry these patties because the pork will release enough of its natural fat for sautéing without the need for extra oil.

In a bowl, combine the pork, salt, pepper, sage, and thyme and mix with a wooden spoon until well blended. Using your hands, shape the mixture into 8 patties, each 3 inches in diameter and ½ inch thick. (The patties can be made up to 2 days ahead of time, tightly wrapped, and stored in the refrigerator. You can also freeze them for up to 6 weeks: Stack the patties, separating them with a sheet of waxed paper or aluminum foil, and freeze in heavy-duty resealable plastic bags. Thaw overnight in the refrigerator before cooking.)

Heat a frying pan over medium-high heat. When the pan is hot, add the patties. Reduce the heat to medium and cook until the patties are golden brown on the bottom, about 6 minutes. Using a metal spatula, turn over the patties and cook until the other side is golden brown, about 5 minutes more. Transfer to paper towels to drain briefly. Serve right away.

MAKES 8 PATTIES; SERVES 4–8

Ground pork, 1 pound

Sea salt or kosher salt, 2 teaspoons

Freshly ground pepper, 1 teaspoon

Fresh sage, 2 tablespoons minced

Fresh thyme leaves, 1 teaspoon minced

Chicken-Apple Sausages

It's easy to make homemade breakfast sausage in your food processor. The secret is to partially freeze the meat—here, lean chicken breast and bacon—before grinding, and to use a juicy ingredient, such as tart apples, to keep the sausages moist.

Working in batches, put the chicken in a food processor and pulse until coarsely ground, 6–8 times. Transfer to a large bowl. Add the bacon to the food processor and pulse until coarsely ground, 3–4 times. Add the bacon and butter to the bowl with the chicken and mix with a wooden spoon until well blended. Add the apples to the bowl.

In a clean spice mill, combine the coriander seeds, fennel seeds, and peppercorns and grind to a medium-fine grind. Add the spices to the chicken mixture along with the salt, nutmeg, and cayenne pepper and mix with your fingertips until well blended. Using your hands, shape the sausage mixture into 12–14 patties, each about 3 inches in diameter and ½ inch thick. (The patties can be made up to 1 day ahead of time, tightly covered, and refrigerated.)

In a large frying pan over medium-high heat, warm the olive oil. Working in batches if necessary to avoid crowding, add the patties and cook until golden brown on the bottom, 3–4 minutes. Using a metal spatula, turn the patties over and cook until the other side is golden brown, 3–4 minutes more. Transfer to paper towels to drain briefly. Serve right away.

MAKES 12–14 PATTIES; SERVES 6–8

Boneless, skinless chicken breasts, 1½ pounds, placed in the freezer for 1 hour

Sliced bacon, ¼ pound, placed in the freezer for 1 hour

Unsalted butter, 1 tablespoon

Granny Smith apples, 2, peeled, cored, grated, and squeezed dry

Coriander seeds, 2 teaspoons

Fennel seeds, 1 teaspoon

White or black peppercorns, 2 teaspoons

Sea salt or kosher salt, ½ teaspoon

Nutmeg, ½ teaspoon freshly grated

Cayenne pepper, ¼ teaspoon

Extra-virgin olive oil, 2 tablespoons

beverages

Tips for a Brunch Cocktail Bar

For intimate gatherings, set up a cocktail bar right in the party room on a counter or side table. In addition to the cocktails, provide nonalcoholic choices for nondrinkers.

Place a colorful runner or place mats on a counter, console table, or sideboard.

Group the glassware, an ice bucket, mixing spoons, and measuring implements on the surface in a logical flow to facilitate drink making.

Arrange the ingredients, such as spicy tomato juice and vodka for Bloody Marys or sparkling wine and orange juice for mimosas, next to the glassware.

Set out garnishes in small bowls: lime wedges or celery stalks for Bloody Marys, halved orange slices for mimosas. Stack cocktail napkins at the end of the bar.

Sparkling Ginger Lemonade

Here, classic lemonade is updated with spicy-sweet fresh ginger and a splash of sparkling water. It's the perfect drink for a summer brunch served outdoors. Look for crystallized ginger in the baking section of well-stocked grocery stores and in specialty-food markets.

Water, 4 cups

Fresh ginger, ½ cup thinly sliced

Fresh lemon juice, ¾ cup (about 5 lemons)

Sugar, ¾ cup, or to taste

Sparkling water, 2½ cups, well chilled

Ice cubes

Lemon slices for garnish

Crystallized ginger, 6 strips for garnish

In a nonaluminum saucepan over high heat, boil the water. Add the ginger, cover, and remove from the heat. Let stand for 5 minutes. Taste and, for a stronger ginger flavor, let stand for an additional 5–10 minutes. Pour through a sieve placed over a glass jar, cover, and refrigerate until well chilled.

Pour the lemon juice into a large pitcher. Gradually add the sugar, whisking constantly until dissolved. Stir in the sparkling water. Taste and add more sugar to suit your taste.

To serve, fill chilled glasses with ice cubes. Pour in equal amounts of the ginger infusion and the lemon mixture, and stir well with a long-handled spoon. Garnish each glass with a lemon slice and candied ginger strip and serve right away.

SERVES 6

Strawberry-Banana Smoothie

Fresh fruit blended with fresh orange juice and vanilla yogurt makes a refreshing, healthy brunch beverage for adults and kids alike. Change the berries to your liking, substituting raspberries, blackberries, or blueberries for the strawberries, or use a combination.

In a blender or food processor, combine the strawberries, bananas, orange juice, and lemon juice. Process until the mixture is smooth, 30–45 seconds. Add the vanilla yogurt and process until thoroughly blended, about 20 seconds.

To serve, pour the mixture into tumblers or large wine glasses. Float a strawberry on each drink and serve right away.

SERVES 4

Strawberries, 3 cups, sliced, plus 4 whole berries for garnish

Ripe bananas, 2, cut into 1-inch pieces

Fresh orange juice, 1½ cups

Fresh lemon juice, splash

Vanilla yogurt, ½ cup

Spiced Iced Coffee

During the warmer months, replace steaming mugs of hot coffee with this aromatic brew flavored with orange zest, cocoa powder, and sweet spices. Take care that the coffee does not steep for too long or the flavors will become too strong.

Coffee, 4½ cups freshly brewed, hot

Sugar, 6 tablespoons

Dutch-process cocoa powder, 3 tablespoons

Cinnamon sticks, 2

Whole cloves, 6

Orange zest, 4 strips, each about 3 inches long by 1 inch wide

Ice for serving

Milk or half-and-half for serving

In a heatproof bowl or large, heatproof pitcher, combine the coffee, sugar, and cocoa powder. Stir thoroughly to dissolve the sugar and cocoa. Add the cinnamon stick and cloves. Twist each piece of orange zest to release the essential oils, then add to the hot liquid. Let the coffee stand at room temperature for 1 hour, stirring occasionally, to infuse the flavors.

Pour the coffee mixture through a sieve to remove the spices and zest, then cover and refrigerate until very cold, about 2 hours.

To serve, fill chilled tumblers with ice cubes. Stir the coffee mixture, then pour over the ice until the glasses are three-fourths full. Fill the glasses the rest of the way with milk and stir well with a long-handled spoon. Serve right away.

SERVES 6

Mexican Hot Chocolate

In Mexico, the traditional hot chocolate beverage is flavored with sugar, cinnamon, and often ground almonds, which lend body to the drink. Tablets made from a combination of these ingredients can be found in well-stocked grocery stores and Hispanic markets.

In a saucepan over low heat, warm 1 cup of the milk. Add the chocolate tablet pieces and stir with a wooden spoon until melted. Add the remaining 3 cups milk and the vanilla bean, if using, and let simmer for several minutes.

Remove the pan from the heat. Lift out the vanilla bean, if using, and reserve for another use. Using a whisk, beat the chocolate mixture vigorously until a thick layer of foam covers the surface, about 2 minutes.

To serve, pour into mugs or heatproof cups, distributing the foam evenly among the mugs. Serve right away.

SERVES 4

Milk or water, 4 cups

Mexican chocolate tablets, 2 (about ¼ pound total weight), broken into small pieces

Vanilla bean, 1 (optional)

Chai Tea Latte

This delicious alternative to coffee is based on a traditional Indian recipe. For the best flavor, infuse the tea with the spices just before serving. You can also serve this drink over ice: Let the strained mixture cool to room temperature and refrigerate until well chilled.

Cardamom pods, 4

Cinnamon stick, 2-inch piece

Whole cloves, 4

Water, 2 cups

Milk, 2 cups

Sugar, 3 tablespoons

Darjeeling tea, 4 bags

Using a mortar and pestle, lightly crush the cardamom, cinnamon, and cloves. In a saucepan, combine the crushed spices, water, and milk and bring to a boil over high heat. Reduce the heat to low and simmer, uncovered, until the spices release their flavor, about 2 minutes. Add the sugar and tea and continue simmering until the tea is infused into the liquid, about 1 minute longer. Strain through a sieve, rinse the pan, and return the tea mixture to the pan.

Place the pan over very low heat and, using a whisk, beat the tea mixture vigorously until a slight layer of foam covers the surface and the tea mixture is warmed through, 1–2 minutes.

To serve, pour the tea mixture into mugs or heatproof cups, distributing the foam evenly among the cups. Serve right away.

SERVES 4

Ramos Fizz

This frothy cocktail was invented by a New Orleans restaurateur in the late nineteenth century and is still popular on brunch menus throughout the South. If you are concerned about the eggs in your area, replace the raw egg whites with pasteurized egg whites.

In a blender, combine the gin, lemon and lime juices, sugar, egg whites, cream, orange-flower water, and crushed ice. Blend until well mixed and frothy, about 1 minute.

To serve, divide the mixture among 4 highball glasses. Fill the glasses nearly to the top with club soda, and dust with nutmeg, if using. Serve right away.

SERVES 4

Gin, 1 cup

Fresh lemon juice, 2½ tablespoons

Fresh lime juice, 1¼ tablespoons

Superfine sugar, 2½ tablespoons

Egg whites, 4 (see note)

Heavy cream, 2½ tablespoons

Orange-flower water, 10 drops

Ice, 2¼ cups crushed

Club soda, about 1⅓ cups, chilled

Freshly grated nutmeg for dusting (optional)

Blood Orange Mimosa

Blood oranges are at their peak from mid-December through March and their distinctive red flesh and juice adds a dramatic flair to the classic mimosa. If you can't find blood orange juice, substitute freshly squeezed Valencia orange or grapefruit juice.

Orange liqueur, ¼ cup

Freshly squeezed blood orange juice, ½ cup

Champagne or sparkling white wine, 2 cups

Blood orange, 1 slice for garnish

Pour 1 tablespoon triple sec, 2 tablespoons blood orange juice, and ½ cup Champagne into each of 4 chilled Champagne flutes or wine glasses. Stir briefly with a long-handled spoon to mix.

To serve, cut the blood orange slice into quarters. Garnish each cocktail with an orange slice quarter and serve right away.

SERVES 4

Classic Bellini

Harry Cipriani of Harry's Bar in Venice invented this peach-flavored cocktail in 1948. You can still find it on the menu there today. For this recipe, you will need only a small amount of the simple syrup; store the rest in the refrigerator for up to 3 months.

To make the simple syrup, simmer the water in a saucepan set over medium-high heat. Add the sugar and stir until completely dissolved. Remove the pan from the heat and set aside to cool the syrup to room temperature. Pour the syrup into a clean bottle, cap it tightly, and refrigerate until needed.

Put the cubed peach flesh, lemon juice, and 1 teaspoon simple syrup in a blender and blend until smooth.

To serve, divide the mixture among 4 chilled Champagne flutes. Gently pour in the sparkling wine. Stir gently with a long-handled spoon and serve right away.

SERVES 4

SIMPLE SYRUP

Water, 1 cup

Sugar, 1 cup

Ripe white peach, 1, pitted but not peeled, cut into 1-inch cubes

Fresh lemon juice, 1 teaspoon

Prosecco, Champagne, or sparkling wine, 2 cups chilled

Grapefruit-Prosecco Cocktail

Prosecco is a light, fruity sparkling wine from Italy that can be found in most high-quality wine shops. Here, it is mixed with fresh grapefruit juice and a touch of orange liqueur to make a simple and refreshing brunch cocktail.

Orange liqueur, ¼ cup

Fresh pink grapefruit juice, ½ cup

Prosecco, 2 cups

Pink grapefruit wedges, 4 for garnish

Pour 1 tablespoon orange liqueur, 2 tablespoons pink grapefruit juice, and ½ cup prosecco into each of 4 chilled Champagne flutes or wine glasses. Stir briefly with a long-handled spoon to mix.

To serve, garnish each cocktail with a pink grapefruit wedge and serve right away.

SERVES 4

Spiced Bloody Mary

A ubiquitous choice on brunch menus across the country, this classic cocktail was reputedly invented in the 1920s in Paris. Each restaurant has its own unique blend of piquant spices and flavorings. Here, the drink features the smoky flavor of ground cumin.

Pour the vodka, tomato juice, and lime juice into a glass pitcher. Add the pepper, salt, cumin, Worcestershire sauce, and hot sauce and stir well with a long-handled spoon.

To serve, fill 4 highball glasses with ice and pour the tomato juice mixture into the glasses. Garnish each glass with a lime wedge and celery stalk and serve right away.

SERVES 4

Vodka, 1 cup

Tomato juice, 2 cups

Fresh lime juice, ¼ cup

Freshly ground black pepper, 2 teaspoons

Sea salt or kosher salt, 1 teaspoon

Ground cumin, 1 teaspoon

Worcestershire sauce, 8 dashes

Hot pepper sauce, 8 dashes

Lime wedges, 4 for garnish

Celery stalks with leaves, 4 for garnish

Brunch Menus

The recipes in this book were developed to complement one another. The examples that follow represent only a handful of the many possible combinations. When planning your brunch menu, keep in mind the character of the recipes: those rich in butter or cheese pair well with those featuring fruit, and combination of savory and sweet dishes balances the menu. In addition, try to combine dishes that have different preparation times: pair a dish that needs to be cooked at the last-minute with something that can be prepared ahead of time.

South-of-the-Border–Style Brunch

Huevos Rancheros 41

Rice & beans

Warm flour or corn tortillas

Mexican Hot Chocolate 113

Spiced Bloody Mary 119

Casual Brunch in the Kitchen

Green Salad with Almonds 23

Breakfast Pizzas 84

Fresh fruit

Self-Service Juice Bar 15

Game Day Brunch Buffet

Red Flannel Hash 77
or Turkey & Yukon Gold Hash 78

Poached Eggs 38

Sautéed Cherry Tomatoes 93

Roasted Spiced Apples 94

Sparkling Ginger Lemonade 110

Spiced Bloody Mary 119

Brunch with Close Friends

Fresh Berry Salad with Mint 22

French Toast & Apple Chutney 58
or Stuffed French Toast 57

Herbed Pork Sausages 103

Chai Tea Latte 114

Grapefruit-Proscecco Cocktail 118

Family Brunch

Buttermilk Waffles 55

Kid-friendly toppings: fresh berries,
whipped cream, chopped nuts

Scrambled Eggs 45

Chicken-Apple Sausages 105

Strawberry-Banana Smoothie 111

Mexican Hot Chocolate 113

Wintertime Fête

Citrus Salad 21

Salmon Eggs Benedict 49

Roasted Rosemary Potatoes 96

Blood Orange Mimosa 116

Make-Ahead Brunch
in the Garden

Cucumber Gazpacho 26

Spring Vegetable Frittata 35

Brown-Sugar
Coffee Cake 62

Spiced Iced Coffee 112

Ramos Fizz 115

Bistro-Style Brunch

Orange-Zest Scones 64

Baked Eggs with Spinach 46

Crispy Pepper Bacon 102

Classic Bellini 117

Index